MonologAye

10 monolog gan bobl Bangor
• • • • • • • • • • • • • • • • • • •
10 monologues by the people of Bangor

Cyhoeddwyd yng Nghymru yn 2024 gan Atebol, Adeiladau'r Fagwyr,
Llanfihangel Genau'r Glyn, Aberystwyth, Ceredigion, SA24 5AQ.

ISBN 9781835390108

Hawlfraint y cyhoeddiad © Atebol Cyfyngedig 2024
Hawlfraint y testun © yr awduron

Syniad gwreiddiol y prosiect: Mared Elliw Huws a Manon Gwynant

Ni chaniateir atgynhyrchu unrhyw ran o'r cyhoeddiad hwn na'i drosglwyddo mewn unrhyw ffurf neu drwy unrhyw fodd, yn electronig neu'n fecanyddol, gan gynnwys llungopïo, recordio neu drwy gyfrwng unrhyw system storio ac adfer, heb ganiatâd ysgrifenedig y cyhoeddwr.

Dyluniwyd gan Owain Hammonds
Llun y clawr: Adobe Stock, Delia_Suvari

atebol.com

I gael caniatâd i berfformio'r ddrama hon, cysylltwch â
BLAS, Pontio, Prifysgol Bangor, Ffordd Deiniol, Bangor, LL57 2TQ.

Rydym yn cydnabod cefnogaeth ariannol Cyngor Llyfrau Cymru a Cymru Greadigol.

Argraffwyd yng Nghymru.

Canllaw Oed: 16+
Mae'r gyfrol hon yn cynnwys iaith gref a themâu aeddfed.

Published in 2024 by Atebol, Adeiladau'r Fagwyr,
Llanfihangel Genau'r Glyn, Aberystwyth, Ceredigion, SY24 5AQ.

ISBN 9781835390108

Copyright of the Publication © Atebol Cyfyngedig 2024
Copyright of the text © the authors

Original idea for the project: Mared Elliw Huws and Manon Gwynant

All rights reserved. No part of this publication may be reproduced or transmitted in any form or by any means, electronic or mechanical, including photocopying, recording or by means of any storage and retrieval system, without the written permission of the publisher.

Designed by Owain Hammonds
Cover photograph: Adobe Stock, Delia_Suvari

atebol.com

If you require permission to perform this play, then please contact
BLAS, Pontio, Prifysgol Bangor, Ffordd Deiniol, Bangor, LL57 2TQ.

Printed in Wales.

Age Guidance 16+
This publication contains some strong language and adult themes.

Cynnwys

Rhagair 4
Foreword 7

The only Jew in the village: **Nathan Abrams** 9
Croeso i'r llwyd: **Leo Drayton** 16
Ffordd Penrhos: **Sioned Griffiths** 21
I like it here: **Beryl Jones** 26
999: **Christopher Jones** 30
Pobl i Bobl: **Esyllt Bryn-Jones** 36
Maes G: **Owen Lee Maclean** 41
I am African everywhere: **Marie-Pascale Onyeagoro-Okonkwor** 48
Alone with myself: **Olaitan Olawande** 52
Harmony, peace, home: **Yelyzaveta Umarova (Lisa)** 57

Bywgraffiadau / Biographies 61

Rhagair: MonologAye

BLAS yw prosiect celfyddydol ymgysylltu cymunedol Pontio, ac rydym yn gweithio yn y gymuned ac ar y cyd â hi. Er ein bod yn gweithio ledled Gwynedd, gan ein bod wedi ein lleoli ym Mangor, yn naturiol, mae'r ddinas yn ganolog i nifer o'n prosiectau, ac rydym wedi cael y fraint o ddod i adnabod nifer o'i thrigolion a gwrando ar eu hanesion. Calon Bangor yw ei phobl, a'i gwythiennau yw ei chymuned, sy'n bair i amryfal o ddiwylliannau, ethnigrwydd, a chrefyddau. Yn dilyn degawd o weithio'n agos gyda thrawstoriad o gymdeithasau a sefydliadau sy'n rhan o'r gymuned hon, daeth yn amlwg bod gan ei thrigolion straeon unigryw a phwysig i'w hadrodd, sy'n ymwneud â'u profiadau a'u perthynas bersonol nhw â'r ardal. Dyma egin MonologAye, a'r bwriad o'r cychwyn oedd cynnig llwyfan a llais i drawstoriad o unigolion, gan roi blas ar yr amrywiaeth anhygoel o bobl o bob cefndir sy'n cydfyw ac yn cynnal curiad calon Bangor.

    Aethpwyd ati i recriwtio unigolion a oedd yn cynrychioli'r amrywiaeth o gefndiroedd, gan fanteisio ar y cysylltiadau a oedd gennym eisoes yn sgil ein gwaith cymunedol. Mae gennym berthynas agos â Chymdeithas Affrica Gogledd Cymru, Annedd Ni, Pobl i Bobl, Prifysgol Bangor, cymunedau LHDTC+ Bangor, mentrau iaith a chymunedau o ddysgwyr Cymraeg, a chymunedau Hirael a Maesgeirchen. Buom yn gwrando ar straeon unigolion o fewn y cymunedau hyn ers blynyddoedd a chawsom ein syfrdanu dro ar ôl tro. Dyma gyfle i rannu blas ohonynt mewn gofod creadigol, diogel a chyhoeddus, ac mae cyfrwng y fonolog yn benthyg ei hun i sicrhau bod lleisiau'r unigolion yn cael eu cynrychioli'n ffyddlon; eu hiaith, eu hacenion a'u harddull.

    Yn dilyn recriwtio ein sgwennwyr, aethom ati i recriwtio mentoriaid profiadol a fyddai'n cydweddu a chydweithio'n effeithiol â phob un. Dan arweiniad y prif fentor Izzy Rabey, rôl y mentoriaid oedd cefnogi a chynnig arweiniad i'r sgwennwyr, yr oedd nifer ohonynt yn amhrofiadol yn y maes ac yn mynd ati i ysgrifennu monolog am y tro cyntaf. Drwy gydweithio, rhoddwyd cyfle i rannu lleisiau nad ydynt fel arfer yn cael eu clywed, gan gymunedau sydd wedi eu tangynrychioli neu unigolion sy'n aml yn cael eu hanwybyddu. A'r canlyniad yw'r deg monolog unigryw, hudolus, a gonest a welir yn y gyfrol hon. Cafwyd noson i'w rhannu a'u dathlu yn Stiwdio Pontio ar y 6ed o Fedi, 2023, pan berfformiwyd MonologAye – rhai ohonynt gan eu hawduron ac eraill gan actorion proffesiynol – a rhoddwyd cyfle i'r sgwennwyr a'r mentoriaid drafod y broses a'r profiad unigryw hwn.

Mae ein diolch yn ddiffuant i'r sgwennwyr canlynol am fod mor barod i rannu eu straeon mewn modd gonest ac agored:

Nathan Abrams
Leo Drayton
Sioned Griffiths
Beryl Jones*
Christopher Jones
Esyllt Bryn-Jones
Owen Lee Maclean
Marie-Pascale Onyeagoro-Okonkwor
Olaitan Olawande
Yelyzaveta Umarova (Lisa)
*gyda chefnogaeth Rachel Jones, Annedd Ni

Ac i'r mentoriaid, am eu harweiniad a'u harbenigedd:
Connor Allen
Alice Eklund
Manon Gwynant
Samantha Alice Jones
Izzy Rabey
Buddug Roberts
Charlotte Williams
Gwion Aled Williams
Manon Wyn Williams

Mae MonologAye yn arddangos lleisiau, ieithoedd, acenion a straeon unigryw Bangor, ac rydym yn hynod falch eu bod yn cael eu cyhoeddi a'u rhoi ar gof a chadw i bawb gael cip ar y gymuned arbennig hon. Mwynhewch eich taith i Fangor Aye; porwch wrth eich pwysau, a phrofwch guriadau'r galon sy'n cadw Bangor yn fyw.

Mared Elliw Huws (Cydlynydd Datblygu'r Celfyddydau)
a Manon Gwynant (Mentor)

Foreword: MonologAye

When I was initially approached by the very brilliant Mared at Pontio to curate this project, I was incredibly intrigued by what the outcomes might be. I am from Mid Wales and I lived in Cardiff for a great deal of my adult life before relocating to London four years ago. I knew next to nothing about Bangor and the creative community there. It was a joy and an absolute privilege to collaborate with so many voices on pieces that were so deeply personal and the core of their experiences of living in this special part of North Wales.

Something I had seen working during my time as Trainee Director at The Royal Court was one-to-one mentorship and dramaturgical support for writers, with the dramaturgs and directors then receiving further support from the literary team. The importance of the bond formed between the mentors and their writers to develop such personal work was vital for MonologAye, but it was also vital that the mentors received adequate support from myself and Mared in terms of how to facilitate the process with the writers. So often, we can cut corners with community-focused projects in terms of the structures and foundations of support and mentorship, and it was deeply important to me that, in terms of this project, we ensured that both the writers and the mentors were cared for consistently throughout the process.

The outcome of this work was the most exciting and wide-ranging collection of voices and experiences I've ever worked on in my career as a director: a hip hopera between a young man and his younger self about the impact of a youth worker; finding a community of Muslim sisterhood at Bangor University; the experiece of making a new home in the North Wales landscape as an Ukranian refugee; the complexity of 'fitting in' being both a Welsh learner and a Jewish Londoner in Bangor; among many many other captivating, delicately and beautifully open and honest stories.

Wales is, and always has been, a nation of diverse experiences, voices and cultures. This is who we are and what makes us so special. My hope with this anthology is that people who share these experiences can see themselves reflected, and for others to have insight into people's lives that differ from their own. This is the power of both the creative process and creative expression. Story sharing is the ultimate act of hope in a world that can often seem determined to divide us.

I hope you enjoy delving into the world of MonologAye!

Izzy Rabey
Lead Facilitator, MonologAye

The only Jew in the village
Nathan Abrams
Mentor: Izzy Rabey

Like that Little Britain sketch from years back, I'm the only Jew in the village.
At least I like to think so.
If I'm not, I'm surely the only Welsh-speaking Jew.
This village is Bangor, North Wales. As its University says, we're positioned between the mountains and the sea.
But isn't everywhere?
It's a city but not quite.
It's as rural as you can get for a North London Jewish boy.
I trade on that image.

My passport says I am British.
'You're not really British are you?' Or:
'When do you have to serve in the Israeli Army?'

I'm not Welsh.
I'm not fully English either.
I sit somewhere in between.
Blurred.
Almost the same, but not quite.

I don't feel English.
Whatever that means.
English people come from Somerset or Devon.
I come from London.
Everyone knows that's not really England.

I come from North London.
I support Arsenal.
'Why don't you support Spurs?'
I'm asked more times than I care to count.
By liberal types who abhor stereotypes.

Do I support Wales?
Having lived here for nearly 17 years, do I get to naturalise?
Your lengthy pause is my answer.

I coach my son's football team.
Clwb Pêl-droed Penrhos.
The team of the dosbarth canol Cymreig.
The crachach.
We got in there because he goes to Ysgol y Garnedd,
the Welsh-speaking school in Bangor.
Like they say, it's who you know.

I get stick from some of the other parents.
Why?
I'm an alien visiting from another planet.
The other parents and coaches all know each other.
From way back.
'He was like that in school… ' they say.
This I can't get over.

My chances of bumping into someone from school are zero.
Even in London.
One of my Welsh friends went to the worst school in Caernarfon.
He ran into one of his bullies.
Well, not literally.
Strolling down College Road: 'What the fuck are you doing here?' he
    heard.
Looking up to see the voice's source, he was transported back decades.

He began to quake.
Feeling those long-buried fears.
'I work at the University.'
'No, you fucking don't.'

This fascinates me.
I have no sense of belonging beyond North London.
My sense of cultural geography is limited.
Because my school was nowhere near my home,
I have no idea what my school bullies are doing.
Nor do I care.

My school was JFS.
Jews' Free Comprehensive.
Joe's Fish Shop.
Pick your preference.
You won't have heard of it.
No-one has.
It never produced the glitterati the others did.
Take the Jewish comedy circuit.
David and Ivor Baddiel, David Schneider, Ashley Blaker, Alexei Sayle, Matt Lucas.
They went to better, private schools.
Well, not Alexei Sayle.

An inner-city London comprehensive in Camden Town, JFS was free.
It wasn't that religious either.
It was suitably located to be mutually inaccessible to the children of London's Jews.
We came from far and wide.
So JFS tried to foster a sense of local community outside of its locality.
We were all Jewish, I think.
Probably not according to today's rules.
But that's another story.

Visit me during my school days, and tell me all Jews are white, clever or rich.
JFS embraced Jews who lived in council-run hotels through to millionaires.
Some of them were thick. Very thick.
Their heritage was European, Middle Eastern and Asian.
Indian Jews, Iraqi Jews, Iranian Jews, Libyan Jews, Black Jews.
But despite how racist the 1980s were, we didn't think about it other than in the nicknames we gave each other.
It was the 1980s after all.
And the 1980s were racist.
The regular lunchtime entertainment of the neighbouring school was to wander down the road to ours.
Standing in the street, they would yell abuse and make hissing sounds and Hitler salutes.
It went on for years. Probably longer than the Second World War itself.
It became part of their curriculum.

Back to football.
I'm also a bespectacled prof.
I don't look like a football player.
Well, not a modern one.
It's the prof thing that is the most alien.
How do I explain what I do to people who may never have been to university?
It's not like they need my services.
Ever.
But I do need theirs.
The other parents come to football in vans.
Not the type of van that is essential in the mountains.
But the type of van with professions emblazoned on the side.
Tilers, electricians, builders, mechanics.
Moving into my house, the removal guy asks if I had done the renovations.

'No, of course not.'
'I didn't think so.'

I feel like a local celebrity in Bangor.
Big fish, small pond.
I know people.
They know me.
Mainly because of my dogs.
The anonymity of London disappears.
I shop with my hairdresser.
I bump into all sorts of people I know.
Through the University, my kids' school, and football.
I'm also the guy who walks up and down Penrhos Road every morning.
With two dogs, waving dog shit at passing cars as I say hello.

Being Welsh and being Jewish are similar.
Israel and Wales used to be frequently compared.
God knows why.
One is short and fat, the other is long and thin.
The population of one is about 3 million and the other at least double, maybe triple, that.
One is surrounded by hostile enemies who wish to destroy it and the other is in the Middle East.

The Welsh-Jewish thing.
Or Jewelsh, as the comedian Bennett Arron calls it.
We both worry about the future.
Will our kids be Jewish?
Will our kids speak Welsh?

Some people think that Welsh came from Hebrew.
That the Welsh are one of the lost ten tribes.
Take bara brith.
You might call it speckled bread.

'Brith' for us is circumcision.
So what the hell is in that bread?
Is it suitable for vegans?
Talking of tips, I was asked if I wanted to stroll up the Moel.
No thanks, I have already seen one.
The mohel (pronounced moel) is the circumciser.

Don't worry if you don't get that joke.
David Baddiel, who is Welsh and Jewish,
used to tell a joke that his half-Jewish friend wore a triangle around his neck and had a twoskin.
The best part was when he waved his hand when no-one got it.
And before you say it, yes, I know;
I look like a slightly anaemic David Baddiel.

One very famous mohel is called Jacob Snowman.
He reportedly circumcised Prince Charles.
And either me or my brother.
Which means one of us has a penis by royal appointment.

Jacob was the older brother of Emanuel.
He married into the Wartski family from Bangor.
And helped to make them world famous.
That would make a great book title. 'From Clocks to…'.

Back to language.
The Welsh Government wants one million speakers by 2030.
I learned Welsh.
Well, struggled to learn Welsh.
I am considered fluent, whatever that means.
But then a five-year-old is fluent.

Welsh is a really difficult language.
Learners panic because there are different sounds.

And hundreds of ways to say 'yes' and 'no'.
And no clear way to learn plurals.
They have no idea what awaits them when they encounter formal Welsh.

It's like learning to swim.
You are given the lessons, the rubber ring, and the armbands, and then chucked into the pool.
You walk along the bottom, thinking this is going well.
So far so good.
And then, oh shit, the bottom drops out and you are left floundering, treading water.
Everyone else lies on their sunbed, drinking a cocktail, and congratulating themselves because they've created another swimmer.
This isn't the way to ensure continuity.
You see, Jewish people have the same problem.
Well, we have many problems but one of them is to ensure that there are enough Jewish people in the future.
Orthodox Judaism doesn't encourage conversion and as only the offspring of Jewish women are considered Jewish, it relies on Jewish men marrying Jewish women.
This creates a clear problem because there aren't many of those.
So we are left in a bind.
The solution is simple. Encourage conversion or at least embrace the non-Jewish partner.
Open the doors.
Let the light and fresh air flood in.
It's the same with Welsh. We don't need more sessions in the pub with other learners.
We need immersion.
Open the doors.
That way, I don't have to be the only Welsh-speaking Jew in the village.

Croeso i'r llwyd
Leo Drayton
Mentor: Manon Gwynant

Y byd mewn bar bach clyd.
Es ti mas neithiwr?
Do, ma' pen fi ben i waered.
Glôb?
Cube.
Queue, freezing, scary bouncer on the door.
Prifysgol. Oedolyn nawr.
4 yn troi yn 21…
…ond dal angen dangos ID.
In, cloakroom, bar.
Bar…
…bar ar ein stepen drws. Uni halls, not bad; my own little box to fit myself inside.
'Let's check it out,' I said to the 7 strangers I now share a microwave with….
Bar Uno. Fel cyfuno – yn dod â homesick students at ei gilydd.
    Wholesome; I like it.
'Do you mean Bar Uno, the one next door?'
Cue darlith i'r Saeson am yr iaith Gymraeg.
Gwaith cwrs due fory;
essay on the neuroscience of bias.
'Us vs Them:
 the troubles of a tribalistic world.'
Côr o wynebau blanc. Colli gwynebau cyfarwydd gartref.
Tequila, sambuca, sours. 'Sheep shagger!'…. Diolch yn fawr.
'Uno.' Last card.
Mis o jôcs am defaid a Tom Jones and 'Oh, what's occurring?'.

Okay.
Sometimes a sacrifice has to be made... or a compromise, as they say.
I can put up with a bit of xenophobia; at least the trans thing wasn't a problem.
'We communicate and interact within the basic framework of us vs them, and we tend to treat them really badly.'
Liquid pink yn llifo i golau'r dance floor. I bet you look good....
Girls, boys, everything in between, between checkerboard patterns ar y llawr.
Checkerboard / chessboard.
Stuck to straight lines,
tied to boxes,
black and white tiles on the floor.
Does that mean we're all pawns?
Moving one square at a time;
guided tours through life.
We all move with the rules of the music.
Do as we're told;
    follow the tempo.
Life is like a game of chess.
Everyone protects the King,
even though he does nothing,
and the Queen is the one who does all the work.
Soldiers for someone else doing as they're told.
Don't stray from where they put you on the board.
Stay in your box.
Free will doesn't mean much anymore.
Traed yn toddi.
Boddi
in a sea of sweat and strawberry vape.
Milkshakes on the classroom carpet and listening to Miss read stories
of mermaids and madmen.
Merched yn diflannu i'r tŷ bach a bois yn hela amser da.
  Anwybyddu boundaries a'r bouncers yn becso dim.

We're all trying to act straight.
Lines get scribbled out,
but I guess the rules don't count to some people.
Blurry lines aren't black and white if you're the one who draws them.
Building towers with Lego blocks.
Cubes were always better,
   or so we thought....
I think I'd prefer a bouncy ball to a box.
I think I think too much.
'Let us think about how our perceptions are affected by that which is imbedded
through systemic racism.'
Chwerthin;
sgrechian o dan fluorescent lights y kitchen. Shots yn sarnu dros
   countertops a sticky jager ar y llawr.
From one box to another. Ciwb. Or Cube, as they say. I can't get mad at
   them for that; it's basically the same.
Steaming. Don't need a coat when the alcohol is sweating out of you.
Ti'n dod i Glôb heno?
Smokers.
Not really smoking, but they're too cool for the music.
Mwgwd o mwg yn cuddio pa mor ugly ydyn nhw. Everyone's fit when
   you're drunk.
Taste of sour cherry and sick mixed with raspberry lipstick.
Chwys, ripped jeans, crys blodeuog.
Pronous lost in translation;
ma 'he' yn hafal i'r ddau yn dibynnu pwy sy'n siarad. Dau neu dwy – it's all
   the same to some people.
Diferyn o edifeirwch ar gwefusau y dieithryn. 'Na i anghofio erbyn y bore.
Bore. Home.
Methu codi. Colli llais. Is that a marching band outside?
Difaru day. Let me stay in bed. Stop the ticking, it's giving me a headache.
   Chwerw a chwantus am cysur Mam a toastie twym. Living on your own
   sucks.

'Nôl mewn. Barbie girls ac American boys.
Toys o chwant a serch.
Music from a year 6 disco thumping through overstimulated ears.
I don't need to hear what you're saying; I'm too plastered to deall anyway.
I miss kids' birthdays with party bags and jelly – shots coming back up ar
    ôl oriau o bouncing up and down ar y dance-llawr.
Bored of this dance floor now;
corneli caeedig yn dechrau teimlo'n oppressive;
teimlo fel mwnci dancing to someone else's songs.
Dwi methu symud yn rhydd pan mae'r bocs yn llawn.
Ti'n mynd i Glôb heno?
Disco ball yn torri'n rhydd; rolio dros y llawr.
Fuck it, pam lai....

Awyr iach;
disgyn mewn i Glôb.
Dwi'n nerfus.
Ddim yn cofio cyrraedd.
Dilyn y disco ball;
trust that it takes you where you need to go.
Cam cyntaf.
Diwrnod cyntaf ysgol gynradd.
4 yn troi'n 21.
Glôb.
Ddim yn gwybod be' 'di be'; dydy'r sffêr ddim yn glir.
Rolio dros y lle i gyd....
Methu mesur sffêr ond ma ciwb yn syth
ac yn syml....
Saib. Ma' mhen i'n tawelu. Llonyddwch yn llenwi fy tu mewn, tra tu fas
    mae'r egni yn ffrwydrol. Sŵn y peli pool yn taro'i gilydd a Bwncath yn
    y background. Mae'r dryswch yn fy mhen wedi diflannu a nawr mae
    'di lenwi hefo cyfeillgarwch cynnes. 'Paid â bod ofn.' Sai'n nerfus dim
    mwy.
Awyr iach. Saib. Gwir saib o'r angen i plesio pobl.

Saib yn y time capsule fach gyda hanes dros y walydd i gyd. Gwynebau yn
   gwenu trwy'r amser ata i.
Saib yng nghatref y bobl Cymraeg; siarad iaith y nefoedd.
Cymraeg wrth y bar: 'Un jwnc os gwelwch yn dda.'
Sgwrsio'n ddwyieithog heb esbonio neu ymddiheuro. Minglo gyda pobl
   newydd ac esgus gwybod be' dwi'n neud.
'Us vs Them?'
Pawb yn deall o le ti'n dod, er bo' ni'n dod o lefydd gwahanol. Dyma'r
   cysur cartref o' ni'n ysu amdano.
A dyma blas melys y jwnc fel blas y squash yn yr ysgol,
lle ma' ciwb yn ciwb a sffêr yn sffêr.
Gwrthrychau yn fy llaw yn lle pethau gwir.
Dydy'r byd ddim yn byw mewn bocsys.
Dydy sffêr ddim yn glir. Rolio dros y lle i gyd. Mynd lle mae moen.
   Doesn't care where you want it to go, only where it wants to go. Dwi'n
   edmygu'r rhai sy'n byw fel peli.
Ni methu rheoli popeth.
Black and white doesn't seem as finite anymore.
Felly croeso i'r llwyd,
where everything's a mess.
Dim bocsys na ciwbiau taclus.
We're all on wheels peddling to keep up with the circle of life.
A dyma ni,
yn trio rhannu'r byd.
Us and them.
Y byd mewn bar bach clyd.

Ffordd Penrhos
Sioned Griffiths
Mentor: Manon Gwynant

Mae Ffordd Penrhos yn ymestyn rhwng dwy rowndabowt: un sy'n arwain chdi i lawr Ffordd Penchwintan tuag at dre Bangor ac un sy'n arwain chdi tuag at yr A55 neu at Gaernarfon. Ma hi'n stretch hir o dai neis sy'n sbio tuag at Eryri ar un ochr a'r Fenai ar y llall. Ma'i ar y ffordd allan o Fangor ac yn mynd tuag at bob man arall. Dyma'r stryd oedd yn gefndir i 'mlynyddoedd cynnar i gyd.

Ma' tŷ ni slap bang yng nghanol Penrhos, ac wrth dyfu fyny, 'oedd o wir yn teimlo fel bo' ni'n byw yn ganol bob dim. Bob bora, 'oedd y lôn yn prysuro, a sŵn y traffic yn rhybuddio bod hi'n amsar styrio a gadal y tŷ am yr ysgol. Finna'n rasio lawr y lôn brysur tuag at y dyn lolipop, yn sgipio a baglu bob yn ail. O'n i bob amsar yn gleisiau i gyd, a'r traffig yn ddim o beth i un mor fyrbwyll a gwyllt â fi, a mam yn ffysian bo' genna i 'ddim sens' ac yn mynnu bo' fi'n gafal yn ei llaw.

Eshi i Ysgol y Garnedd, dim ond tafliad carrag o tŷ ni – yr ysgol oedd yn curo ym mhob 'Steddfod, 'nôl pan oedd o'n yr hen adeilad. O'n i wrth fy modd bod pawb ar ben ei gilydd drwy'r amser, a bod rhaid i chdi gerdded drwy'r dosbarthiadau er mwyn cyrraedd unrhyw le. Doedd na ddim byd mor exciting na ca'l mynd â neges o athrawes ar un pen o'r adeilad i un ar y pen arall. Busnesu ar bob un dosbarth fel o'n i'n mynd, clywed sŵn yr ysgol yn byrlymu... gafr binc binc binc... bore da Mrs Jones, bore da bawb... un dau dau, dau dau pedwar, tri dau... ond doedd dim amser i aros – ro'n i'n ei heglu hi'n ôl rhag cael ffrae gan Mrs Edwards.

'Oedd plant Penrhos i gyd yn mynd i Ysgol Garnedd, ag 'oedd y tai o 'nghwmpas i'n llawn ffrindia'. O'dd fy ffrind gora' yn byw reit dros ffordd. Roedd gennan ni bob matha o gynllunia' i adeiladu pont o un ochr i'r llall;

y ddwy ohonan ni wedi cael llond bol o orfod disgwyl am riant i'n helpu ni i groesi, a mor annoyed bob tro 'oedd un o'r mamau yn galw ni o un pen i'r llall.

Mewn 'chydig o flynyddoedd, byswn i'n cerdded 'chydig (ond dim llawer) pellach i Ysgol Tryfan. Roedd yr holl genod oedd yn byw ar y Ffordd yn cerdded 'efo'i gilydd, yn stopio wrth bob tŷ fel oeddan ni'n mynd.

Yn Tryfan, dechra' gweld bywyd tu hwnt i Benrhosgarnedd. Gafon ni gyfarfod plant o Felin, Maes G, Llanllechid.... Yn sydyn, 'oedd bywyd yn llawn trips ar y bws i dre Bangor i edrych am ddillad a ca'l hot chocolates yn Gerrards, neu neidio ar drên i Cineworld yn Llandudno – am Pizza Hut a Tango Ice Blast. Heb orfod dibynnu ar drafnidiaeth cyhoeddus i gyrradd yr ysgol, oedd trena' a bysus mor exciting. Doedd na ddim cyfla gwell i ga'l clwad y gossip heb orfod poeni am rieni yn gwrando yn y sêt flaen neu yn y 'stafell drws nesa.

Mewn 'chydig o flynyddoedd, nath yr outings droi'n yfed mewn cae yn Felinheli a partis mewn clwb rygbi yn G'narfon. Roedd teenagers Caernarfon, Brynrefail a Bethesda yn cynnig llwyth o bosibiliada' newydd, a'r alcohol yn g'neud pawb yn ddigon hyderus i gyflwyno eu hunain. Dyma annibyniaeth, a do'n i methu ca'l digon ohona fo.

Roedd Penrhos, hefo'r rhieni yn ffysian a'r holl wyneba' cyfarwydd, yn dechrau teimlo'n reit fach erbyn diwedd fy arddegau. O'n i wedi derbyn gymaint o gariad yn fa'ma dros y blynyddoedd, ond mi o'n i'n barod i ddianc. Fa'ma oedd y lle oedd wedi'n magu fi, ond fa'ma oedd y lle oedd wedi'n mygu fi hefyd.

Yn ddiamynedd ac yn ysu am antur, dyma wneud penderfyniad hollol boncyrs – Prifysgol Leeds.

Dwy awr a hanner i ffwrdd oedd Leeds yn y car, ond 'oedd o'n teimlo fel mod i wedi cyrraedd Mars. Sgyrsiau 'efo pobl oedd ddim ofn brolio eu bod nhw'n 'top of their class' yn English. Nightclubs ar gornal bob stryd a gwahoddiada' i 'afters' gan bobl 'efo stamina lot mwy na ma' alcohol yn rhoi i ti. Mynd ar goll ar y ffordd i Tescos ryw ben yn fy wsos cynta', a jest â marw isho dod adra. 'Oedd traffic Penrhos yn teimlo fel hwiangerdd i gymharu hefo heavy metal y ddinas. 'Oedd 'na rhywbeth oeraidd am y prysurdeb; roedd gan pawb rhywle i fod tra mod i'n teimlo hollol out of place.

A'r iaith.

O'dd bob sgwrs yn teimlo'n awkward, a finna'n baglu dros fy ngeiria'.

'Sioned.'

'Charlotte?'

'Sioned.'

'Sinead?'

Sioned.

Ond, 'efo amser, nesh i neud cartra' i'n hun yn y ddinas fawr wyllt. Mi nes i ddod yn rhan o brysurdeb Brudenell Road, Call Lane a'r Headrow yn yr un ffordd ag oeddwn i'n rhan o brysurdeb Penrhos. Roedd gen i lefydd i fod a chynlluniau i'w gwneud gan yrru sŵn y ddinas i gefn fy meddwl, fel 'oedd sŵn Penrhos wedi bod. Daeth 'na rywbeth braf am beidio adnabod pawb ar y strydoedd; rhyw ryddid o fod yn hollol annibynnol. Daeth gwynebau cyfarwydd i ganol y bobl ddiarth hefyd, gan gynhesu'r torfeydd oeraidd.

Daeth sgyrsiau oedd inevitably yn cychwyn 'efo cwestiynau am Gymreictod yn gyfle i siarad am hunaniaeth hefo pobl newydd, ac nid dim ond yn rhywbeth oedd yn marcio fi yn wahanol.

Doedd dim Mam a Dad i edrych ar fy ôl i ar y lonydd mawr, na ffrindia' cyfarwydd i fynd ar y bws na'r trên hefo fi. Mi oedd yn rhaid i mi ddysgu sut oedd g'neud petha' ar ben fy hun, a dysgu sut oedd adeiladu cartra' fy hun, fel oedd Mam a Dad wedi creu i mi ar Benrhos.

O'n i'n teimlo fel person hollol wahanol. Yn sydyn, o'n i'n bwcio flights ar ben fy hun i fyw yng Nghanada, neu'n trefnu trips o gwmpas Awstralia, ac wedi casglu'r hyder oedd ei angen i fod yn hollol self-sufficient.

Ond wedyn daeth y galwad fwya' scary eto. Cynnig swydd 'nôl adra.

Am y tro cynta' 'rioed ar ôl graddio, doedd na ddim cam nesa wedi ei osod i fi. O'n i'n teimlo fel bod fi'n free falling, ac mi o'n i'n desbret i ffindio lle a rôl i fi fy hun eto.

Ond ai mynd 'nôl adra oedd y peth gora' i mi? 'Oedd fy ffrindia' i gyd yn cynllunio eu cyrsiau masters yn Leeds, neu'n dechrau eu gyrfaoedd yn Llundain a'u tripiau mawr i Asia a De America. Ai dyna ddyliwn i fod yn g'neud? Be' os fyswn i'n colli'r holl hyder yna wrth symud adra? O'n i'n cymryd cam yn ôl?

Er yr holl amheuon, nes i ddychwelyd i Ffordd Penrhos lle mae'r traffic bora dal yn wallgo', a'r plant yn dal i redeg tuag at yr ysgol, a'r rhieni'n dal i ffysian drostyn nhw. A tŷ hyfryd Mam a Dad ar Ffordd Penrhos; lle sydd wastad wedi bod yn llawn sŵn a phrysurdeb a chariad, a groesawodd fi 'nôl heb gwestiwn wedi fy holl anturiaethau.

Ond mae'n rhyfedd – dydy'r tai o 'nghwmpas i ddim yn llawn ffrindia' dim mwy, a mae na rhywbeth eitha' unig mewn byw mor agos at y rôl o'n i'n chwarae cynt, heb allu ffitio'r mowld hwnnw mwyach.

A dyma gychwyn swydd yng Nghastell Penrhyn – castell mawreddog ar ochr arall Bangor. Mi oeddwn i wedi ymweld ychydig o weithia' o'r blaen, ond yr unig beth 'oeddwn i'n medru cymryd sylw ohono fo ar y pryd oedd pa mor enfawr ydi o. Wrth i mi grwydro'r castell yn fy wythnosa' cynta', ac arfer gyda'i faint, dwi'n gweld arddangosfa 'Beth yn y Byd'. Mae'n canolbwyntio ar eitemau sydd yn y castell sy'n gwreiddio o bob ban o'r byd. Cromen llawn adar lliwgar wedi eu stwffio o Affrica, papur wal wedi ei beintio yn Tsieina, a bocs bach gwyrdd o Jamaica oedd yn cynnwys manylion am gaethweision oedd yn llafurio i greu'r cyfoeth sydd i'w weld ym Mhenrhyn. Safle o syndod a sarhad.

'Nôl yn y brifysgol, nes i arbenigo yn hanes y Caribî. 'Nesh i 'rioed sylweddoli bod yr hanes hwnnw mor agos at adre.

Mae'r Bangor dwi'n adnabod erbyn hyn yn wahanol iawn i Fangor fy mhlentyndod, a dydy hynny ddim jest oherwydd bod Topshop, HMV a Debenhams wedi cau. Drwy fy ngwaith ym Mhenrhyn, dwi'n dod i adnabod Bangor hollol wahanol. Dyma Fangor o fyfyrwyr awyddus a chymunedau amrywiol. Dwi'n ffindio'n hun yn ail-ymweld â llefydd dwi'n gwybod i mi eu gweld yn fy mhlentyndod a'u gweld mewn cyd-destun newydd, fel Hirael, oedd yn ddim ond 'y darn o Fangor wrth ymyl y pwll nofio a'r pier' yn fy mhlentyndod, ond erbyn hyn dwi'n gweld ardal hefo hanes difyr a chymeriad cryf.

O fewn y Bangor yma, mae lle i mi. Does dim angen i fi ffitio union mowld fy mhlentyndod; gallaf dreulio amser mewn llefydd na fues i 'rioed ynddyn nhw pan yn ifanc, a chyfarfod pobl newydd sy'n dod â persbectif ffresh. Ond mi fedra i hefyd ddal ymlaen i bethau sy'n bwysig i mi yma, fel ail-ymweld hefo rhai o fy hoff lefydd, ail-gysylltu hefo hen ffrindiau, a threulio amser hefo'r pobl wnaeth fy magu i, hefo dealltwriaeth newydd o pa mor werthfawr oedd y magwraeth hwnnw.

O'n i wedi bod mor awyddus i weld a phrofi gweddill y byd, heb sylwi bod digon o'r byd i'w weld ym Mangor, dim ond i chi wybod lle i sbio.

I like it here
Beryl Jones
Mentor: Buddug Roberts

Crikey. I know I'm supposed to be thinking about something else right now, but I can't stop thinking about a panad. Can I get a panad here? Dying for a panad I am. Could you go make me one? Thanks; is that a bit cheeky? If you think that's cheeky, I'd even tell them if it's a bad panad, and ask for another one! I'm just honest, you know? That's one thing you know about me already….

Gosh, lots of you here yeah…. I get a bit nervous; no, serious now! And now you know another thing about me… I get nervous talking to lots of people. You wouldn't believe this; it's true, I swear. Even my family – doesn't matter who. I had to do a speech on my 70th birthday a few years ago and I got so nervous, even though they were only my friends and family.

Since we're all gathered here nicely, I'll tell you a bit more about me then, yeah? I live here. I've lived here for years. But I'm not from here. I was born in Liverpool; yeah, I know – I'm a Scouser! I moved here to Caellepa to live with my Granny because of the War. I was too young to even remember the War though. I still live there, here today, in the same house. I didn't see my parents a lot, obviously. Because of the War, see. But even though I didn't see them a lot, I remember a lot of the little things, you know? The little sweet things from those days. Gosh, nice place Bangor was in those days, you know. All the shops were better then, you know. Better than they are now. I only go to Asda now because there's nowhere else to go….

But back in the day, you had the bakery, the butcher and the best of all – sweet shops. My favourites were the Dolly Mixtures from Woolworths. And ice cream – ice cream for 50p! Could you believe that you could get an ice cream for 50p – well, anything for 50p – back then?

I used to work in Woolworths – it was my first job. I was a volunteer in the stock room and then the canteen later on. I loved it. Can't stop thinking of them Dolly Mixtures now… makes me think of being a little girl again, playing high jumps, hop-scotch, rounders and hide and seek in the big grass in Roman Camp. Being mischievous, you know? Not misbehaving; just being kids, you know? Giggling in the grass whilst our parents were looking for us. I'm awful once I get the giggles, you know. I remember once I was in the church choir. I sang by myself as well – I was good, you know; I was only 13! 'Oh little town of Bethlem' – I remember all the words… but I'm not singing to you, no way! But yeah, I remember having the giggles badly when people were reading in church – we weren't even supposed to speak never mind laugh!

I love thinking of the good old days… looking through old papers and photo albums and stuff. But I do cry sometimes when I look at pictures. I'll cry quite a bit; I get quite emotional, you know?

I am happy though – you know you just cry sometimes when things get hard and you miss someone.

No-one likes to talk about Covid no, but gosh that was hard. It was hard for everyone yeah, but like really hard because I depended on people, you know? I was the same when I lost my parents – I depended on them so much. I still miss them.

But yeah, with Covid, I couldn't go shopping on my own and someone else had to do it and you know when you just want specific things and no-one else gets it no?

Nobody could even come to my birthday – Rachel came to see me outside with a mask. I was so grateful – you have no idea. Thing is, I didn't understand Zoom or anything like that, but I did actually see a service from Ebenezer Church on it.

When I was young, my uncle Bob bought me a present – a doll, dolly, in a big box and I remember it always sat in the box – I wasn't allowed to take it out and actually play with it, you know? I felt like that doll in the box. I was stuck in the house.

The same house I've lived in for around 70-something years….

I used to travel a lot to places, you know. My parents would take me to places like Cricieth and Tenby, and I remember playing bingo, having Christmas dinner and everything. My aunty, my mother's only sister, lived in Chester, and I went to see her from time to time and we'd go to a fancy hotel and we'd go for a walk with the dog (there's another story with that – I lost it, but it found its way home). I was allowed to go on my own sometimes as well – I remember my mother said to my father, 'Let her go'. He gave me money and I went on my own to see my aunties and cousins in London.

I still travel quite a bit as well. I've been to see my brother in the Wirral – went for a couple of days there – and I'm supposed to go to Dublin on a trip, which is so exciting. I love going to new places and I love coming back here.

I like going out, you know – I'd rather be out than sitting in. I go for lots of walks; I've started walking to Annedd Ni now, you know.

I do knitting as well – blankets and stuff. I like knitting – it gives me something to do; passes the time away; therapeutic. I can do a square in a night, with a glass of wine in hand – 'medicine'! I've made a blanket for Denice that works in Annedd Ni, and bonnets and stuff.

Like you can probably tell, even though I did depend on people, I am independent; independent like my grandfather. I remember him going to Beaumaris on the bus all on his own to the shops… like me.

When I said earlier I only go to Asda to shop, you'll never guess what happened to me there. I was just walking, talking, doing my shopping. And I just got chatting, you know; I'm like my father like that – I'll make friends with anyone. My mother was shy, but my father could speak to anyone – like me. But anyway, I met my now friend Jackie – met her in Asda after a chit chat and then, long story short, I got an invitation to her wedding with her partner from Ireland. I was shocked; I couldn't believe it!

I love things like that, you know. I enjoy my life now – I have a lot of friends. I have one in Port Dinorwig I met in the 60s – every other Saturday, we went places together. I went to see her on Saturday a few weeks ago and she was in bed. When I saw her, I cried – I didn't recognise her, but I'm happy I saw her, even though it upset me; it still reminded me of the happy days.

Funny how things change, isn't it. But also how many things stay the same.

Family and friends mean the world to me.

I'm the only one in my family who remembers all my great aunties. I remember they used to call me Maisy; so did a lot of people, because I reminded them of my mother.

One of my aunties, aunty Nelle, wrote a poem – it was for my parents' wedding and I remember when my cousin sent it to me, I cried all day; I broke down. It's so special to me because, even though my family's scattered everywhere, it's like having a piece of them with me all the time. I like thinking of the last two verses….

'So off they rode in the sunset,
Actually they went by train,
Back to the land of his Fathers
Bangor – in the rain!'

'And now some years later,
Family and friends have come to say,
On your special anniversary,
Many happy returns of the day.'

I get so emotional reading it even though I've read it a thousand times by now. This is so important to me and my family. A lot of people come and go here, in Bangor, like. My family is scattered everywhere – London, Cheshire and Wirral, and all sorts… and I'm here; I've always been here. And I like it here. People 'ride off and return' and I'm here – like Bangor – changing all the time, getting older. Bangor's getting quieter – I'm not too sure if I can say the same about me…. But I can say one of us is getting better, nicer, prettier by the day…. But I won't tell you who!

999
Christopher Jones
Mentor: Gwion Aled Williams

Christopher looks away from the audience when answering his calls but addresses the audience when recalling his memories.

Automated Voice: 999. What emergency service do you require?

Caller: Ambulance please.

Christopher: Ambulance Service. What's the address of the emergency?

Caller: Ysgol Hirael, Orme Road, Bangor, LL57 1AY.

Christopher: Did you say Ysgol Hirael?

I remember one time, my primary school, Ysgol Hirael, had a float in the annual carnival. One year, it was pirate themed, and the next year we all dressed up in the colours of the World Cup and went on the back of a trailer, singing songs whilst the long queue of parade marched down towards Beach Road. The whole city was buzzing with excitement as people prepared for a day of fun. I had been looking forward to the carnival for weeks; I had saved up my pocket money and was determined to have the best time possible. My first stop was the candy floss stall. I took a bite, and the sugary sweetness melted in my mouth.

I then headed over to the games area where I tried my luck at winning a prize. After a few failed attempts, I finally managed to win a small teddy bear. I went for the rides where my friends and I spent time on the bumping cars, the sizzler, and the waltzers. The carnival was great; I carried on going there every year until unfortunately it stopped. I was a first aider there once with St John's Ambulance, and because of that opportunity in the carnival, I was asked to be a first aider at Ras y Wyddfa, other carnivals, and different events, and held the flag on remembrance day.

PAUSE

'Could you repeat that address for me?'

Caller: Wyt ti'n siarad Cymraeg?

Christopher: Yndw. Ailadrodd y cyfeiriad plîs.

Caller: Dwi'm yn siŵr. Tu allan i siop tua diwedd stryd fawr Bangor. Mae'n dweud 344 uwchben y drws.

Christopher: Dwi wedi gyrru linc i dy ffôn i what3words. Agor y linc a deu'tha fi be ydy'r geiriau.

Caller: Panad. Cadeirlan. Siopa.

Christopher: My favourite shop in town was the Playmobil shop; well, I say town – it's closer to Hirael than anything. The Playmobil shop is now split into 2 shops – Linda's Barbers (who used to cut my hair when I was little) and All Sewn Up (where I once got my school uniform). I remember the times I visited the Playmobil shop with my Mam and older brother. We were always so excited to go and had been talking about what we were going to get. As soon as we arrived, my eyes would widen with excitement as I saw the colourful displays of Playmobil toys. We walked around the shop, admiring all the different sets and figures. My living room floor was once covered in Fireman Sam toys, and Playmobil vehicles. My favourite was the bus! Right across the way was Valla's chippy. It's still here to this day – a family-run business that's moved from generation to generation for 80-odd years. I personally have a special connection to Valla's – my Nain, Auntie, and Mam once worked there. They were very close friends of the Valla family; as a matter of fact, my Mam is named after Mammy Valla, the first generation of Vallas, Rosa Eluned Jones. I used to sometimes go to Jo Valla's house after school – she'd pick me and her nephew and my school friend Harry up, and we used to have so much fun with her and the dog, Sasha.

PAUSE – Christopher begins to turn away from the audience, but then has a thought and quickly has a point to share.

Also, remember when you could walk into Poundland and things would actually be a pound? Try that in 2023 – you won't get very far!

PAUSE

'We have prioritised your call. You can expect to wait approximately 30 minutes for an ambulance to arrive and can I just confirm you said Pontio Arts and Innovation Centre, Deiniol Road, Bangor, LL57 2TQ?'

PAUSE

> Pontio! Some might not know, but I remember when Pontio was a little building in the high street, where I believe the cat charity shop is now. It was this small little area – fast forward to the present day where the University funded this massive building. I have had the privilege of watching Pontio grow as a company, and I am so happy that I have been a part of the vision, especially with BLAS. When this very building was a construction site, Ysgol Hirael and Ysgol Glancegin from Maes G performed with opera singer Bryn Terfel. Glancegin sang, and Hirael signed the lyrics of 'Anfonaf Angel' – you can find it on YouTube! I remember wearing my brother's blue wellies, a hard hat, and a high-vis, standing where the open space outside the studio is. I remember I cried because I didn't manage to get an autograph, but luckily Mared, my drama tutor and Arts Coordinator of Pontio, saved the day, took my blue book, and got Bryn Terfel to sign it for me! I've done so much with BLAS – I've been to Bridgend for an awards ceremony, made a film, been on the red carpet, acted in many shows, helped out backstage with many shows, been an Ambassador for the Circus Feast before Covid, and much much more.

PAUSE

> 'Stay on the line; I've located you now.'

PAUSE

> As a child, I remember the excitement bubbling within me as my family and I went on a stroll to Bangor Pier.

As we approached the pier, my eyes started to water, mainly 'cause it was windy, but also knowing in the back of my head that we lose the longest pier battle to Llandudno. I remember people of all ages strolled leisurely, their laughter and chatter intermingling with the noise of the seagulls. I remember we had ice cream, a scone in the cafe and we went crabbing, and as I looked down through the gaps between the wooden planks, I caught glimpses of the restless waves crashing against the pier's support beams. I still go there to this day. Not long ago, I went for a walk with this girl I know, Kayleigh – she likes jellyfish so we went on a little hunt. We seen a few, but they were all the same type of jellyfish. It was nearby, so we walked up to Roman Camp – you know, the biggest beer garden in Bangor – and sat down on the bench and looked over towards Anglesey, and behind us was Bangor Mountain.

PAUSE

'Don't worry, I'm here with you; I'm not going anywhere.'

PAUSE

I've grown up in Bangor and for me Bangor is home, and will always be home, wherever I might end up living. I was born into a Welsh family so obviously dwi'n gallu siarad Cymraeg. Nes i fynd i ysgolion Cymraeg, 'neud fy'n driving test, fynd i Coleg Menai, cael job cyntaf fi i gyd yn Bangor. Dwi wedi mynd o Ysgol Hirael i Ysgol Tryfan, ac wedi cael diploma yn Biomedical Science yn Coleg Menai. Job cyntaf fi oedd Fresh Colleague yn ASDA. Yn 18 oed, nes i cael promotion i job Section Leader / Duty Manager – something I will always be proud of! Rwan, dw i wedi cychwyn career newydd yn gweithio fel EMS 999 Call Handler i'r Welsh Ambulance Service. Pan o'n i'n fach, mi o'n i isho gweithio fel Paramedic felly mi oedd cychwyn job newydd yn gweithio i'r Gwasanaeth yn rêl dream come true. Be' dwi'n trio deud ydi, I'm a Bangor lad aye, born and bred!

PAUSE

Christopher: Okay, you take care now. Bye bye!

Automated Voice: 999. What emergency service do you require?

Caller: Ambulance please.

Pobl i Bobl
Esyllt Bryn-Jones
Mentor: Manon Wyn Williams

Set: Cadair freichiau, teledu, pram, eitemau cegin i'w didoli i focs, sgrîn yn y cefndir er mwyn taflunio'r negeseuon testun.

O'n i wastad ishe dod i Fangor.

Cyrraedd y Coleg Normal yn '91. Tic.

O'n i wastad ishe byw ym Mangor, ar Ffordd Penrhos, credwch fi neu bido. Tic-ish. Sai'n byw yn bell o' 'na!

Dwi'n caru Bangor. Roedd cyrraedd Bangor yn ddeunaw mor exciting. Gallwch chi gadw eich Gyrdydd. Ych, fi'n cofio mynd am gyfweliad 'na – cyrradd ar y bus, dod off y bus, a gwbod yn syth dim hwn odd y lle i fi.

Ond Bangor, o'n i'n gwbod yn streit. I'd arrived. Llwyth o siope, tafarne, take-aways. Gosh, ma' Bangor 'di newid. Siope 'di cau: Debenhams, Top Shop, H&M i gyd 'di mynd. A dim byd yn eu lle. Ffenestri 'di bordo lan; popeth mor jyst llwm a rili digalon. Ond roedd 'na bobl; pobl o bob man. Fast forward i 2023, ma' dipyn mwy o bobl 'ma. Ma'r bobl fi'n sôn am wedi gorfod dod yma – o'dd dim dewis 'da nhw.

Ffôn symudol yn gwneud sŵn. Mae hi'n darllen y neges. Mae'r neges yn ymddangos ar y sgrîn.

> Hia Esyllt. Ydy hi'n bosib rhoi shout out am deledu?
> *Teipio ateb*
> Ydy, dim problem; 'na i 'neud 'wan.

Neges Facebook

Annwyl gefnogwyr, rydym yn chwilio am deledu sy'n derbyn Firestick. Os fedrwch chi helpu, cysylltwch â ni drwy e-bost. poblibobl.bangor@gmail.com
Dear supporters, we are looking for a TV that accepts a Firestick. If you can help, please contact us at the above e-mail. Diolch o galon am eich cefnogaeth barhaus. Thank you for your continued support.

Setlo ym Mangor. Gwaith, teulu, ffrindie. Byth yn teithio'n bell. Eniwei, s'dim raid i fi deithio yn bell, pan fi'n byw mewn lle mor braf, plus ambell i drip 'nôl i'r de, a Lerpwl yn 'itha aml y dyddie ma 'fyd. Ni'n falch bo Io wedi setlo 'na. Lle gore i gerddor, medde nhw. Ni mor lwcus. I mean, ma' Aberaeron yn lyfli (ddim yn yr haf falle!). Ond co, ma' popeth 'ma – y mynyddodd a'r môr. Chi'n gallu ca'l trên i rwle. Na, actually, chi ddim y dyddie 'ma, ond chi'n gwybod be sy' 'da fi. Ma' 'na rhanne rili hardd 'ma – y pier, a'r cherry blossoms yn Ashley Fields. A faint o weithe fi 'di cerdded rownd Caeau Briwas…? Ond ma'r dre ei hunan yn depressing, fel lot o lefydd. Digalon.

Yn y Capel o'n ni yn eistedd yn y gynulleidfa 'da Mam – blynydde 'nôl. Beth o'dd hi? Tua 2016, yn yr haf. A'r pregethwr yn cyhoeddi bod criw Pobl i Bobl yn dechre cwrdd yn y festri am ddwy awr bob wythnos, i helpu ffoaduriaid i ymgartrefu 'ma. Yma. Ym Mangor. Pwniad gan Mam: 'Go on, bydde ti'n lico neud rywbeth fyla.' Bydden, bydden i yn, actually.

Felly un nos Iau am 'wech, lawr a fi. On i'n hen gyfarwydd 'da'r adeilad, ac yn athrawes Ysgol Sul 'na, ond o'n i'n timlo bach yn nyrfys. Eniwei, mewn a fi. 'Hi, how are you? I'm Laura.' 'Hi, I'm Es – Esyllt, but that's a bit of a mouthful; people call me Es. I heard about this meeting in Chapel.'

Mwy a mwy o bobl yn cyrraedd: Cymry, Saeson, dysgwyr, Syriaid. Pob un mor wenog, yn cyfarch ei gilydd 'da 'Salam Alaikum'. Fi'n cofio just edrych o gwmpas. Lot o 'How are you?', golchi llestri, siarad a deall bod ambell un yn athro. 'Me too.' O'dd rywbeth 'da ni'n gyffredin. Ond oedd e rili? Fi yn saff fan hyn ym Mangor, a nhw... *(saib mawr).* Fel o' nhw'n timlo?

Cyrradd gytre a ffaelu stopo siarad am y peth – siŵr bo' fi 'di hala pawb yn nyts, ond o'n i 'di caru fe. Mynd bob wythnos a trial helpu'r bobl i ddeall tamed bach o Saesneg – sôn am Bangor, y siope ar Ffordd Caernarfon. A dysgu 'chydig o eirie newydd: 'Sukraan' – diolch.

A wedyn mynd i 'sgubor Dr Zigs yn wythnosol – bob nos Fercher am 'wech ar y dot – i sortio'r dillad. Ac mi oedd tomen o ddillad wastad yno. Pobl leol yn rhoi yn hael. Pobl Penrhos, pobl Hirael, pobl Siliwen, pobl Garth, pobl o'r Ynys, bob man. 'Nath hi ddim cymryd yn rhy hir nes i fi ga'l Huw on board, a Mam pan o'dd hi lan, 'whare teg iddi. Un peth 'nath rial argraff ar Mam o'dd gweld un gŵr o Syria yn plygu'r dillad. Na, dim jyst plygu nhw, ond anwesu nhw. 'Weles di fe; weles di fel o'dd e'n plygu'r dillad?' Achos yn aml iawn, o' ni gyd, dim jyst fi, yn citsho rwbeth lan – 'Ych, bin.' Ne'n gweiddi ar ein gilydd, 'Be na fi 'da hwn?' 'Just put it in there.' Ond o'dd e mor ofalus.

Sortio'r dillad mewn i fagie, ac o'dd 'na LOT o fagie. Women's tops small, medium, large; women's trousers small, medium, large; women's coats small, medium, large; a'r un peth i'r dynion a phlant. O'dd dim lle i droi. Pan o'dd y bagie'n llawn, trefnu i heirio fan, a ffindo rhywun o'dd yn fodlon dreifio – Huw sawl tro – a mynd â nhw i warws mawr yn Northwich lle o' nhw'n cael eu rhoi ar loris anferth yn barod i'w hallforio i'r camps yn Lebanon a Gwlad Groeg.

Teimlo fel oes yn ôl a popeth sy' 'di digwydd ers 'ny – Brexit, Covid.

Fi'n cofio pan gwmpodd Kabul – wytchan y teledu, chi'n cofio? Y bobl yn rhedeg a'r eroplên yn dal i fynd…. o'dd e'n erchyll. O'dd rhaid neud rywbeth. Kait yn gweld bod elusen Care4Calais yn trefnu bod paciau hylendid yn cael eu paratoi ar gyfer y rhai oedd yn ffoi ac yn cyrraedd yma. O' nhw literally yn cyfro wal yn y dining room, a dim just tŷ ni. Sawl un o'r pwyllgor. Ac o'dd hi'n Covid ar y pryd.

Sŵn ffôn symudol – e-bost ar y sgrin.

> Helo. Newydd weld eich neges ar Facebook. Mae gynon ni deledu i chi. Dydy hi ddim yn fawr iawn ond mae'n gweithio yn champion.
> Gadewch i mi wybod,
> Gyda diolch.

Ma' pethe'n ddrud; 'sdim arian 'da pobl. Ond ma' 'na bobl rili ffeind i ga'l. Faint o weithe ma' rywun 'di mynd i Felin i 'ôl ffrâm gwely, neu i'r sticks i nôl ford. A fi'n credu bod pobl yn falch o fedru helpu – y teimlad 'na o neud rywbeth. Mae gan bawb stori a ma' gwbod bod eu pethau sbeshal nhw yn mynd i rywun bydd yn eu gwerthfawrogi yn jyst… wel, ma pawb yn elwa. Fi'n gwybod o'dd Mam a fi'n rili falch bod beic dad wedi mynd i rywun yn un o'r camps yn Cyprus. Buodd e'n y sied am bron i 20 mlynedd ac o'n i mor falch bod stori'r beic yn parhau, a bo' ni heb just ei werthu neu mynd â fe i'r tip.

A'r apêl am pethe cegin. My god; o'dd 'stafell sbar Manon yn llawn dop. A criw ohonon ni'n mynd 'na i'r bedroom i sorto pethe mewn i household 1, household 2, 3, 4, 5, 6…. O'dd system dda 'da ni. Casglu setiau o gyllyll a ffryc, llwyau a llwyau tê mewn i 4, 5 neu 6, gan ddibynnu ar maint y teuluoedd, ac o'dd unigolion hefyd wrth gwrs. Setiau o fygiau, platie, casserole dishes. Wedyn galwad gan y Cyngor i ddweud bod teulu ar y ffordd; rywun yn nôl y bocs a mynd â fe. Fi'n credu bod Manon 'di cael ei llofft 'nôl erbyn hyn!

Cofio ni'n trefnu i fynd â'r Afghans i Bangor Tandoori ar yr high street er mwyn dod i 'nabod nhw'n well. Ma'n rili galed weithe, pan 'dos dim iaith yn gyffredin. Lot o' ni'n dibynnu ar Google Translate! O' nhw mor ddiolchgar.

Sgrolio'r ffôn a neges yn ymddangos ar y sgrin.

Hello you. Thank you for your kindness.

Erbyn hyn, ma'r bobl ma'n ffrindie, a fi'n gallu stopo a siarad 'da nhw. Fi'n falch iawn o 'na. 'Mond ddoe weles i rywun pan o'dd Huw a fi'n cerdded i Morrisons. Huw yn ysgwyd llaw: 'How are you? How's it going?'

'Good thank you. See you soon.'

CLIP NEWYDDION – RHYFEL WRCAIN

Mis Mawrth 2022; galwad ffôn gan y Cyngor. 1, 5, 20, 60… mwy o bobl yn dod o hyd ac o hyd. O'dda' nhw'n traumatised, ac o'dd e'n anodd i ni ar brydie. Dim iaith, ond gwên, cwtsh, cyffyrddiad llaw, dagre yn aml. Do'dd dim angen geirie.

Mynd â chriw o Wcraniaid ar y bus i Lanberis. Gymrodd e awr, ac o' ni'n gorfod sefyll yr holl ffordd. Ble arall ni 'di bod? Cwm Idwal – o'dd hwnna'n dda. Cofio un ohonyn nhw'n golchi ei hunan yn y llyn. Dyn neis oedd e. Nidodd Huw a fi off y bus 'da fe yn Porth Penrhyn, a mynd â fe i'r lle pysgod. Chware teg, gath e beth am ddim. Credu mai music journalist o'dd e'n arfer bod. O'dd e'n lico rai o'r un bands â ni eniwei. Weles i fe'n Marks cwpwl o wythnose 'nôl.

Ffôn symudol yn gwneud sŵn. Mae hi'n darllen y neges.

> Hi Es. How are you? Do you fancy a panad in Kyffin? We can discuss our new fundraiser?
> Ideal. I've just got to pick a TV up from Llangefni, then I can meet you there. 2?
> That's fine. Maybe we can have a walk to the pier afterwards?
> Great. See you later.

Gorffen gyda fideo byr am y paciau hylendid yr oedd PiB yn gyfrifol amdanynt.

Maes G
Owen Lee Maclean
Mentor: Connor Allen

Can be performed by one or two actors.
The stage is blacked out. Nothing can be seen. Rowan comes on, curiously looking around. The audience catches his attention.

Rowan: Who are you?
What? What?

Getting in the audience's face.

> What are you looking at?
> Look at the head on that guy!

Me: Wow, wait, pause.

PAUSE

> Years ago, I would have reacted to this;
> see, I was just like you.

Rowan: Ha ha ha, no chance old timer.

Me: Hang on then;
let me rewind and take you to the start.

Rowan rewinds and lies down. A light comes on and he complains about the brightness.

Rowan: What's that light? Aaahhh!

Me: Staring from the womb,
        In the emergency room,
        A son of Bangor was born into the eye of one of life's storms,
        Blurry vision, muffled sounds,
        From an incubator, until 10 days later.

        Years pass on from one to terrible twos,
            The toddler phase on the sofa in the evening while watching Blue's Clues,
            Filling my face on potato smiley faces and some spaghetti hoops.

Rowan dances around miming RUN DMC.

    1997. Six years of age with the world at my feet.
    Mam would be dancing round the house while giving it a clean.
    It's like that blasting by RUN DMC.
    I'd be in my own world holding the remote control thinking I was an MC.
    In the special needs unit due to learning difficulties.
    Red folders made us stand out for the wrong reasons; we might as well have had a Post-it note saying 'bully me' stuck on our backs, so of course it was hard to always stay on track.
    On a daily basis, a lad would take my toys and any other belongings I would have off me, pushing me around, grabbing any opportunity to put me down, until I go boxing and gain the confidence to stand up for myself.
    Now the tables have turned.
    He tried me again – this time I say enough is enough. Punch him square in the mouth and learn that he's not so tough as he falls to the ground like a big sack of spuds.

Rowan plays out getting pushed against a wall and then punching the air.
Rowan cheers.
Party sounds play out.

>A new millennium party in almost every house and street – I was nine at the time.
>
>Not too many years after, I'm starting secondary school; getting into some scuffles while in and out of trouble. I go from a timid kid in primary to the class clown.
>
>Summer schemes, discos and river clean-ups with Paul Hockaday and the gang. Youth club would be open four nights a week and then we had another hang-out area for Friday nights called HLC.
>
>Paul was always the patient one who rarely raised his voice and would always go the extra mile to help out in his role – a bit of a pushover, but we all grew to respect him and a few more of the role models we had for our generation.
>
>2009. Turning 18. No clue of what life had in store for me; not seeing the value in my community. Until advice from the elders, such as Paul and Andy, sunk in.

Voiceover of the advice given fills the space.

>Partying on weekends in our mate's caravan was where it would go down – it literally became the talk of the town. We went on to hitting the pubs, clubs and raves – they would often turn to days of getting into a state.
>
>Passionate to MC and get on the mic, I start getting regular slots at local raves – I was feeling blessed.
>
>But then I come to learn it was just about getting in a mess, and I realize I have so much more to get off my chest. So a few years on, I give the raving a rest.
>
>Who knew this messy time would come back and haunt me and make me depressed.

PAUSE

>Unlucky 2013, the curse of cancer came,
>   My grandad and aunty Lil became ill then diagnosed on the very same day,
>   Within six months, they'd both passed away.
>
>I go to music college and find so much more confidence in my craft. The tutors were helping me to see my potential but I couldn't commit to the full course as I was just setting up and toying with the idea of running music and lyric-focused workshops for youths in and around my community. I go from a year of being a student to being asked back to the college to facilitate the odd workshop. Buzzing that I'm in the right environment, I would talk to Paul about the tracks I was working on. Being a trade unionist and musician, he would drop the odd inspiring idea for track concepts.
>   Many times we spoke about how much a community studio would benefit the area.
>   There's a new light – our estate is one of 10 picked to be supported by the Building Communities Trust with funding to facilitate and develop beneficial things in the community. Paul rounded up a load of residents and wanted a few of us to represent for the younger generations, so we go to the first meeting thinking this could be the chance our area needs.

Lighting change – represents the shift.

>2017. One of the lowest I've ever been. Mental health really took a toll on me.
>After a few weeks, I get a call.

SOUND OF RINGING

Owen, bad news, it's Paul....
What, what's happened?

He's taken his life.

We knew he was ill; he even joked about euthanasia if his results showed cancer. But we didn't see the depth behind the joke.

Time froze and the blood in my veins felt as if it was running cold – cancer again.

Why...?

Rowan paces back and forth.

No, no, no; this can't be true.

This can't be the time he goes. We had so many plans. I'm only just learning the ways and becoming close friends from our weekly catch-ups.

We now have this new support coming with there starting to be cuts from councils and further up, but the person who was really driving and pushing for good things and making them happen is now gone. No-one will ever be able to replace Paul – he literally used to take us to job interviews and question us on the company, and prepare us for the interview too. No-one had the level of passion he had for this area, especially from away, but this estate became his family.

I never understood the impact he had on my life until he was gone.

That legacy must live on through all of us who he's pushed to be strong.

Bangor and Maes G mean the world to me,
But it's so disheartening to see,
Rates too high on this empty street,
It's like our city's been swept from our feet.

Too many cuts over the years in youth sectors; have the council no clue of the repercussions? It's like we are going backwards in time. The big wigs are all talk.
    How could they possibly say they are invested in the future if the people of the future are left to a point of almost neglect.
    Someone needs to clean up this mess; they should have known this would cause an effect.
    Now it's 2023 and we're back to that scene.

Rowan kicks off with the audience again.

Rowan: What you looking at?
             You're lucky I don't slap you about man.

Me: Chill out mate – you're not going to gain anything good from acting this way.

Voiceover from the skies – the same advice as previously.

Rowan: What you on about? Pfft, you're clueless.

Me: Trust me. I've been where you have been. I've walked in your shoes and they don't last long walking those rugged paths.

Rowan: What's the point in being good? No-one really cares anyway.

Me: You'd be surprised how many care about you, and if you start caring for others, it will always come back in some way, shape or form.

Rowan: Ohh shut up will ya'.

Me: Look, if it wasn't for the guidance I'd had growing up, as well as much more, then what path would we really be on? The right path or the wrong one?

Rowan and I stand side by side looking at each other for a brief moment and then part ways either side of the stage, walking our paths, whichever they may be.
I walk back on and perform the 1991 track to wrap it up.

I am African everywhere
Marie-Pascale Onyeagoro-Okonkwor
Mentor: Charlotte Williams

(With hands akimbo) I am African everywhere… most times wished I was darker. I always wanted darker skin. I asked my mother, 'Can someone apply anything to the skin to have a "sweet black" glow?' I want to be sweet black. See the beauty-endowed Khoudia Diop, the melanin goddess from Senegal.

The colour of my skin is my healthy and prominent signature *(showing off the skin of my arm)*. I am proud of it.

I am African. I have a philosophy attached to the last four letters of the word AFRICAN (I can). I can… this is my mantra. My true identity *(I raise my right hand)*. I am different. I love that I am different. Put yourself up with excellence, attitude and endeavour.

Leaving Manchester Airport behind and moving *(inward to outward stretch of the hands)* through the outskirts of North Wales made me pinch myself. The trees *(looking on both sides, showing off imaginary trees)* on both sides of the road allowing the fresh breeze of the sea to nestle leaves. I travelled back to the highways of the south-east of Nigeria. The warm sun on your face *(closed eyes with face upward)* and patted by the fresh breeze through the trees. The hills and mountains go up and down *(up and down movement with the hand)* like a roller-coaster.

Bangor, Gwynedd hit me with a nostalgic realisation: 'Am I in Port Harcourt, Rivers State in Nigeria?' *(lowered open hand and looking side to side)*. So similar, the south-east and south of the country are adorned with trees of different heights having unending conversation *(pretends to have a conversation)*. The water surrounds the land as a fortress *(circular movement)*. The waves, a remainder of the beauty of the shores. The rains can go on the whole day into the nights; the only difference is we see it as a blessing *(looks up slightly with hands up)*. We go about our businesses despite the showers from Heaven. I pinched myself several times. Yes, there are similarities in the climate but it's much colder. Here in Bangor, the skies are not always the happy blues. Maybe that's why rainy days are referred to as terrible *(thinking)*. I am still an African everywhere… *(strike my chest)*.

Walking down Bangor High Street, with straight, tall buildings clustering together competing for space, and looking uninterested. Unlike back home where buildings can range from little, short, and tall, with varieties of colours of the rainbow. Spaces are for the children's 'hide and seek'. Variety is the spice of life. Amidst this, the warm faces smiling back at you with a 'Hi' melt all the plainness away *(smiling)*. That's more like it: 'I am fresh and new in your country. People should take care of me.' I am home from home, where everyone greets politely but here it is very brief. 'Ekele bu nchacha ihu.' 'I sana chi?' Your language is your true identity. There are things that can only be said in your language and understood. 'Noswaith dda.' 'Cyfarchion.'

Suddenly, a hit with a shopping trolley! *(Sigh.)* We are hospitable; a smile should be real, not…. Just like the ticket man at the train station who expressed displeasure that I am African.

Black or brown, bold and beautiful… *(hands akimbo)* I am African everywhere….

Just as there are different colours of skins, people have different attitudes in life. But is the soul the same? What is the colour of your soul – isn't it the same colour as mine?

Academic study brought me to Bangor… like many before me and many to come. My dream was to use my academic skills to impact the community positively. 'I'll make the best of it': that was my little promise to myself *(emphasis on self)*. With the scourge of lockdown, unforeseen situation at Uni and coming into Uni late due to visa misunderstanding, I lost sight of this little self-promise *(sad; breaks down in tears)*. I missed my children who were still in Africa. This was distracting… *(holding the phone to my ear)*: 'Mummy, when are you coming to tuck us into bed?'; 'We stay up late hoping to see you walk through the door.'

I struggled… *(sigh; struggling motions)*; low marks… *(sigh)*, harsh words from some tutors…. Then she came along with some words of comfort *(looking hopeful with bright eyes)*. It was as if she was seeing through my eyes; her speeches were so warm. I felt better. She will always be my best tutor. Sara, you have a beautiful soul.

I made it, graduated and happy.

I put the tears behind me *(wiping my eyes)*. There are some who take care of you and some who don't. What is the colour of your soul?

My children are here on Menai Terrace *(hugging self)*. I say to my children, we are home away from home. We are going to offer the people the beauty of our culture because we are Africans everywhere – *(talking sternly)* don't forget where you are from and keep your language going.

They say we take, but I know we give… *(pointing to self)*. We don't give a smile and don't mean it. We confront wrong but don't back-stab. Your belief about us is wrong. Many who put aside prejudice have come to see the truth. They regret the wrong indoctrination.

Down memory lane in history, we have always given: *(slightly waving)* the plantations, our priceless mineral resources, our man-power to date, and much more. Look at me *(emphasis on self)*. Two of my art works in honour of Kyffin Williams's Aber Falls at Oriel Môn – I brightened the white and black concepts to embrace the warm happy African colours; volunteer work with St John's Ambulance; The Book Project; The Fish Princess / Y Bysgodes as a Pontio trainee tutor at the African society centre; and other contributions.

Just like the ticket collector, he misunderstands us – why does he pick me out as if I didn't pay? Maybe he thinks every black or brown person means fraud. PREJUDICE *(angry tone)*. My dignity matters. What is the colour of your soul – isn't it the same colour as mine?

I am 'Agu na-eche Mba' *(the amazon women stand)*. The lioness that protects her pride with all her essence. I am 'Ada Ugwu, Ije-o-ma' *(taith dda)*. I am African everywhere….

We are not helpless or oppressed. We make a difference and offer it in a good way. Come to the house of an African and you will always have food.

It is our pleasure to offer it. They say we take, but I know we give…. I am African everywhere… 'Agu na-eche Mba'… *(warrior-like stand with hand held high).*

Alone with myself
Olaitan Olawande
Mentor: Samantha Alice Jones

Alone with myself. Myself. The one I fear the most. Exhale, inhale – damn, wrong order. Guess I'm nervous? Nervous, or am I excited? I guess these emotions come from the same place, it's just how I choose to channel it. It's a fright to be away from my family, alone; I'm so far from home. This is where trust begins. Trust between myself and my instinct. I wonder if we'll do well. I'll try turning my wriggling caterpillars into bold butterflies and be ready to soar into new adventures. Get ready to use my new-found wings after crawling on the ground for so long. I AM ready to use these wings to carry me to freedom, growth, and fulfilment. The wings I've finally been gifted – yet I had to wait a while. The wait felt like forever, but now the time has come.

I wonder what comes next in this land so far away from the home I know. A new language, a new landscape; yes, it's all so exciting. The air feels different – it feels light, and the sounds and the scenery tickle my senses. It's a delight to be away from the 'city', or at least that's what I used to call it; in a strange way, I've always been a rural girl. I've now been given the chance to show the world what this rural girl can do.

Searching and wondering. *Wondering where I'll find my tribe. Searching for my purpose.*

I stumble on what feels like home. Their laughs and their voice sound all too familiar. 'The music and the food aren't all too different – my people', I think to myself.

The Afro-Caribbean Society – ACS for short; people with similar memories and parallel experiences to mine. A new subculture is born, one intertwined with Western and African values. I think I'm making more friends here. However, I'm too shy; whenever it's time to talk to people, I'm getting tongue-tied.

'To the pub!' Ah, this can't be the only place to socialise. It's a world far from my own; my spirit doesn't feel it belongs here. There must be another way.

Girls' Night! That's a fun idea; a place for women to talk, connect, vibe and laugh. It's time to organise and prepare; a guest list, food and games are a good enough start. Let's hope people will turn up, is the message in my heart. Purpose-driven invitations are the way to the soul. The intention has been set, the seed has been sowed, and what flower might blossom from the ground. Food check: the meat must be halal; a space that's inclusive of my Muslim needs. Alcohol-free zone; let's see where we get. It's new, it's fresh – well, not for me. It's different to what they're used to but the same for me.

Alhamdulillah: an event to remember. The music's playing, people are dancing, chatting, eating. All women. It's loud, it's warm, it's inviting and exciting. This is where I enjoy being; where my people are; some of my people. I guess it is easy to make friends. Someone to talk to and let down my walls. Someone to take account of and point out my flaws. A friend? No, a sister. I've found a sister in Islam.

'Have you prayed?' 'Are you eating halal?' No, yes, maybe…. Argh, I'm not the perfect Muslim! I'm sorry, okay? I still don't know who I am outside the imposed beliefs exerted on me. I'm not the perfect Muslim but I'm trying to get there. Am I eating halal? I mean, sis, we're in North Wales – I would have to go vegetarian. I can't live without my meat – I'm African; that's all I know. You know what, I don't even care. I'll do what I want when I want; you know, I'm getting there. The point is, I'm trying my best – get off my case! Just leave me to make my choices and be on my way!

Wait…. What do you mean you're leaving? Where are you going? Please don't go; I have no-one else. Ha ha – let's laugh, joke and talk…. I see. I won't hold you back my sister in Islam. Wherever you are in the world, we'll remain connected and intertwined. I just can't believe it; I have to start again.

Enactus – what the hell is that? They explain it again and again but I'm still kind of lost. 'Just come to room 29 and try it out', and so I did. 'A place where students can create social enterprises based on problems in the local community.' This is cool. This is fun. I'll present at nationals too! I'll be the competition manager! I'll be society president. This is great; I get to help the community and create meaningful change!

What about my change? What about creating more meaning in my life? Why can't I help myself? The more I help others, the more I self-discover, and I know I need more. I need more of something. I'm forever grateful for the experience but something is still missing.

I'll spend some time with myself. A day in my room should do it. I think two days is fine. A week would possibly fill me up. 'I need a month off the grid.' Better yet, is there a way to pause the world and hop off for a second?

A dark room; closed doors. I'm feeling lonely. I'm feeling lowly. Is this what they call depression? I don't want to move out of bed. No-one try to contact me, no-one try to call me – I won't pick up. I know I'm not doing it right, but this is the best I can do. No-one can see me like this. I'm too horrible to look at. I'm broken, I'm breaking – down, I'm spiralling. I'm a mess. I feel the way my room looks. I can't get past this feeling that I am not worthy. They ask why I help people so much. Why I'm compassionate, supportive, and understanding. I give some generic replies, but the real reason is that it's easier to help others than it is to save myself. That's why when you speak, I'll remain silent. I'll listen and be here because I know it's what you need. Like a seed needs water and sunlight, I'll feed you your nutrients in my garden.

I wish I had someone who would listen, or at least I wish I trusted people enough to share with them.

It's too dangerous outside. Life-threatening. Stay safe. It's funny how I have survival instincts. It's not like I don't want to be here, it's just I wish there was an easier way to co-exist and co-habit with the voice in my head. Pause. Everything is in suspense. Sorrows. Silence. I could be next. Closed eyes. Slowed breathing. I'm still here. Still standing; still contemplating. The doors open. You can go outside. I can step outside into the big wide world. Wear a mask. Keep your distance. Sanitize and take a test.

It's a blank canvas. So many unknowns. Who do I want to be? A better question is, who do I NOT want to be anymore? How do I want to present myself to the world? I want to be here for me. I'm worth saving. I want to wear a hijab, because if anything it's a reminder that I'm proof that my Maker will always believe in me, even when I don't have what it takes to believe in myself. When I wear my hijab, I want people to see a Muslim woman empowered by her faith.

I'm going back to uni – my bachelor's degree is done. I made it out, somehow. Now I want to do a masters. Bangor is one of five unis that offer the course I'm looking for. It's a sign. I got accepted, with a fully funded scholarship too. Ya Allah, your plan is the best plan. Back to Bangor. As someone new and improved. I wonder if I'll make any friends – I wonder if I'll find any sisters.

I want students on campus to SEE me when I start work, as part of the res-life team. I want them to feel comfortable enough to ask me if I know where the prayer room is, or what halal food is nearby. Community. How do I fit my prayers around my lectures and seminars? How do I manage fasting during exam season? Sisters; I want sisters in Islam. After losing one, I noticed the importance of being spiritually grounded. Sisters on a similar journey to mine. Navigating uni life as a practising Muslim woman.

Ramadan – let's start there and invite people for iftar. Let's break our fast together, eat, pray, laugh, and reflect. And again, at Faheedah's house, and again at Imaani's kitchen, and again at Rizwana's accommodation. Yes, it's an open invite; tell a friend to tell a friend. The more people, the more blessings. May Allah be pleased with us and our efforts.

Eid approaches and everyone looks to me to organise something. 'Let's do it; go big or go home! Treborth gardens – everyone come dressed to impress and then afterwards we'll go to CocoVanille on Bangor High Street. Wake up Eid morning and attend morning Salah at Bangor Islamic Centre.' Call the cabs; everyone gets in! We've arrived. The air is light, and the breeze gives me a gentle kiss. What a delight! On the way back to CocoVanille, walking down the high street from the Bangor clock tower, we hear 'You all look so lovely', 'Is someone getting married?', and

'You're all dressed so well'. 'Eid Mubarak!' we reply as we make our way to the dessert parlour. What a day; let's get some rest for part two of the celebrations tomorrow!

The afternoon comes and the skies clear! It's BBQ time. The sun is shining, and the BBQ is sizzling with chicken tenders on the grill. Fruit punch. Zobo and Chapman are the drinks available so you can fill your cup, your essence, your soul. You fasted in Ramadan and now let us feast. Dance to the melody – the oonts and oonts of the afro beats. With sunglasses and sunscreen, the girls come prepared, to take pictures on the picnic mat, cameras out, and strike a pose in their straw-laced beach hats. All the men gather around the grill, pop cans open, gist and chill. The food is ready; it's time to chop. Laughs and loudness; I've heard this tune before – home. I've created a home. We may be from different bloodlines, but we've created one family; a home away from home. Like the one I've always known. This one is warm, and its warmth soothes the soul. One more year left of uni, and I've finally found my people. I don't want them to ever feel alone – alone like I did when I first arrived. At war with themselves choosing between deen and dunya, I hope they come to find peace; a piece of their culture and faith in the space we've created. We may not be blood but we're faith related. One Ummah, one God, so we each have an everlasting bond. Tighter than inside a molecule leaving no space for fear, anger, or doubt. No room for drought, or drainage of the soul. The cup that was once half empty is now twice as full. Pouring and overflowing with love overspilled. Our greater purpose to our brothers and sisters has now been fulfilled. And when I leave uni, I want the community to strive. Without my presence, I want it to remain alive. Alive in their hearts, mine and many more to come. That's it; I've decided to make it a society! We'll call it Sisters In Islam. Let's register at the SU and make it official. Tie the knot; make our vows to do what's best. It's been approved. Alhamdulliah, 'The pages have been written, and the ink has dried'. 'Which one of your Lord's favours do you deny? Did He not find you lost and then guide you?' Or certainly He did, to sisters in Islam society; to success and community, may Sisters In Islam forever live.

Harmony, peace, home
Yelyzaveta Umarova (Lisa)
Mentor: Alice Eklund

If someone would ask me how I would describe Bangor in three words, I would say – harmony, peace, home.

My name is Lisa. I came from Ukraine due to terrible war in my country, but despite the fact of how horrific this situation is, I was lucky enough to meet loads of amazing people and see a bunch of incredible places. Bangor became one of these places.

Four years ago, before the war started and everything was still peaceful and safe, when I was travelling to mountain region of Ukraine with my classmates, I decided and was 100% sure – I want to live in a place like that.

I always loved my city, which is full with busy people always being in rush, but this is exactly what made my visit to mountains very special and life-changing – a huge contrast between two significantly different lifestyles.

During the trip, I discovered absolutely new senses – the smell of forest and feeling of how wildlife fills the whole area. It was autumn, and every time I'd make a step, I could feel a satisfying rustle of leaves under my feet.

It felt like this place was never ever touched by humans before, and it's hard to compare this feeling of natural innocence to anything else.

The animals are the owners of the land; I was reminded of that each time I heard the wolf howl in the middle of the night.

Our hotel was located by a wonderful lake, and even though the colour of water wasn't a crystal blue like on perfect pictures from internet, it was one of the most beautiful lakes I have ever seen. Nature that surrounded us was unbelievably different from what we used to see. That's when I realized my soul wanted to stay here forever, if only I had a choice.

And guess what? I always knew that Universe listens to me, but I could never imagine how literal it will be. While escaping war, first place I was located in was French Alps. Five months after, I had to move to Bangor.

I felt like I was chased by mountains since then.

Universe, probably, really loves me. But let's put all the jokes aside.

Harmony. Surrounded by breathtaking landscapes; nature in all its manifestations and multiple spring sunsets I would never forget. I was finally able to have peace in my soul.

Evenings spent by the seaside or somewhere high in the mountains took a huge part in healing my PTSD and decreasing my anxiety.

I am so grateful to have a place in this world that resembles my home and happy years before I had to go through the roughest months of my life. It is very valuable to have a space where your best memories revive with a new power and I gain more energy and hope since; it really is heartwarming.

Peace. Bangor became a place where I could forget about everything and run away from my doubtful thoughts, hide in the spots where no-one would be able to find me, take my ukulele or drawing equipment, and just sit with relaxing music on. That is a type of therapy for me.

Did someone ever notice how special people in this area are?

Me and my ex-boyfriend once came to the bar and a group of people joined us, starting to teach us Welsh.

It was a bar with a beautiful open terrace in the corner of Holyhead Road called 'Belle Vue'. You can meet different types of people in this place – from locals that come here for a pint or watching football games, to someone who is very very Welsh.

There was a girl talking to her friends in Welsh, which caught my attention immediately. I personally like the way this language sounds a lot – I am also in love with Welsh names, the way that they sound, the way they sit in your mouth, and as you can imagine, this lady also had a very Welsh name. Soon after we've seen this group of people, they joined us and started a conversation and giving us lessons of their language. That was truly amusing. I really wanted to learn, so it's almost like they read my mind. It was nice to have people talk to us and want to teach us their language.

When weeks after I accidentally met them again and I asked if they remember me, the girl they were trying to teach Welsh to, they simply answered: 'Ah, we do this to everyone.'

Isn't it amazing how passionate these people are about their culture, area and language?

Home. I visited a lot of towns and cities in Wales, and what really impresses me and makes me feel united with Welsh people is how patriotic they are. They also know what it's like when your language is being limited, society underestimates the importance of your history and cultural identity together with independence is trying to be taken away from you.

I think most of you know about the prejudice from England's government towards Welsh people; I think that's why these people are always 'ready to fight'. They know their value, they know their history and they realize their uniqueness, such as Ukrainians understand theirs.

As an Ukrainian, I fully understand how important it is to remember your background.

That's why I am so proud of Welsh people being able to stand up for their culture.

I am definitely not here to teach you your own history, but I think it's important to mention. You may know that just like Ukrainian, Welsh has been banned by government. Oral traditions that had survived centuries were lost. And only after years of banning the language and discriminating against its speakers, in 1967, a very important piece of legislation was introduced: the Welsh Language Act. It gave rights that allowed people to use the Welsh language.

I can compare it to the Russification of Ukraine – that was a body of laws and other actions undertaken by the Imperial Russian and later Soviet authorities to strengthen Russian national, political and linguistic positions in Ukraine. Ukrainian language was eliminated from state institutions, schools, and all spheres of social activity of the people. After almost 100 years of pressure, in 2014, Ukrainian language started to revive.

I can see a strong connection here, and I know how hard it is for countries to be overtaken by other governments.

Did you also know that one of Ukraine's biggest cities, Donetsk, owes its creation to a man from Merthyr Tydfil called John Hughes who, towards the end of the 19th century, left the Valleys to start a new life in what was then one of Imperial Russia's industrial centres? He founded a steel plant and several coal mines in the region, and the town was named Hughesovka or Yuzovka (Юзовка) in recognition of his role.

As you can see, there are so much more similarities between my hometown and Wales than anyone could even imagine.

Wales is very special. Bangor is very special. And Ukraine will always be very special to me.

Bangor has a rich history behind it. It's not a brand-new city full of skyscrapers and business centres where there is nothing left from the past; it has changed a lot throughout the whole timeline before we could see it the way it is now.

No doubt, this is a rare, quiet and cozy place and these are one of the things that make it so unique.

And this is why, if someone asks me how I would describe Bangor in three words, I would say – harmony, peace, home.

Diolch.

Bywgraffiadau / Biographies

Nathan Abrams
Nathan Abrams is originally from north London but has lived in North Wales with his two children and two dogs for the past 18 years. When he's not teaching at Bangor University, he is busy trying to improve his Welsh and exploring the Jewish history of the area.

Leo Dayton
Mae Leo yn awdur llawrydd o Gaerdydd sydd yn aml yn ysgrifennu am ei hunaniaeth a'i brofiadau fel dyn traws. Roedd yn astudio ym Mhrifysgol Bangor pan ysgrifennodd y fonolog. Dechreuodd ei yrfa ar ôl gweithio fel cyd-awdur ar y nofel 'Robyn' yn y gyfres i bobl ifanc 'Y Pump', ac, ers hynny, mae wedi gweithio ar nifer o brosiectau megis y ddrama 'Dy Enw Marw' gydag Elgan Rhys sy'n rhan o ŵyl Nation Theatre Connections 2024. Mae ei farddoniaeth wedi ei chynnwys yn y gyfrol 'Curiadau', y flodeugerdd LHDTC+ Gymraeg gyntaf, ac yn 'Room/Ystafell/Phong', sef prosiect ar gyfer awduron o Gymru a Fietnam a gyhoeddwyd gan Parthian Books.

Sioned Griffiths
Cefais fy ngeni a fy magu ym Mangor, ac roedd Cymru a Chymreictod yn rhan hanfodol o fy hunaniaeth, ond yn dilyn cyfnod yn astudio Hanes Rhyngwladol yn y brifysgol, daeth creu cysylltiadau ehangach yn fwy pwysig i mi. Bellach, dwi'n gweithio yng Nghastell Penrhyn lle y mae edrych yn agosach ar y straeon rhyngwladol yn rhan bwysig o fy swydd. Yn fy amser sbâr, dwi wrth fy modd hefo cerddoriaeth

o unrhyw fath, mynd i Côr Dre a gigs o bob math, neu jest yn cael tonc ar y piano.

Beryl Rita Jones

I have lived in Bangor nearly my whole life after moving here as a toddler during the War, and although I've not long turned 80, I'm proud to say that I still live in the family home.

You'll often see me walking around Bangor; I have many friends locally and they all know I never say no to a cup of tea!

I have lots of wonderful memories from my childhood and of Bangor over the years, and I loved having the opportunity to share these as part of MonologAye.

Christopher Jones

Having been born in Bangor, I have lived here all my life. I've known the ups and downs of the city, not only from my personal experiences, but through my family's eyes as well. Generation to generation, Bangor is in my blood. From Caban, to primary and secondary school, and then college to a job – I've done it all in Bangor. Dwi'n Bangor lad aye!

Esyllt Bryn-Jones

Yn enedigol o Lanarth, Ceredigion, rydw i wedi ymgartrefu ym Mangor ers gorffen coleg bron i 30 mlynedd yn ôl. Yn 2016, dechreuais wirfoddoli gydag elusen leol, Pobl i Bobl, yn cefnogi ffoaduriaid mewn amrywiol ffyrdd; rhywbeth y cefais fwynhad mawr o'i wneud. Ar ôl elwa a dysgu o'r profiadau wrth wirfoddoli, rydw i bellach yn gweithio yn y maes ac yn dal i deimlo'n angerddol dros y ffoaduriaid sydd wedi ymgartrefu yn ein mysg.

Owen Lee Maclean (aka A Gent Orange)

A Hip Hop facilitating artist, producer, writer and poet. Born and raised in Maesgeirchen (Maes G), one of the largest council estates in Wales.

Most of my expressive work is reflections of experiences I've lived and seen others around me go through, with a hint of a riddle and a rhyme for a reason. Lyricism and Hip Hop have helped me grow and adapt as a person.

Marie-Pascale Onyeagoro-Okonkwor

Marie-Pascale Onyeagoro-Okonkwor studied an MSc in Clinical and Health Psychology at Bangor University. She is a multi-tasked caterer with the brand name Baram Afro Pop-up Kitchen, who has started making her presence known in the business world. She was involved as a trainee tutor in the project that gave birth to the first children's book written by the children of the North Wales Africa Society, 'The Fish Princess'. She creates artworks that consider the visually impaired appreciation of the arts, and her works have been displayed at Oriel Môn on Anglesey, and at Wrexham University. Marie-Pascale is a wife, and a mother of three daughters.

Olaitan Olawande

The name Olaitan means 'wealth never ends'. Olaitan is a multi-passionate creative who loves to explore her essence through self-expression. She loves writing, including poetry and thought pieces. She is currently embarking on a journey to further harness her creativity by creating a new community for female creatives called 'The Multifaceted Babes'. She loves play, dance, expression and connection. She believes in the power of communities and the collective to promote wellness and joy. She would describe herself as intuitive and spiritual. The piece she has written explores her spiritual and self-explorative journey during her time at Bangor.

Yelyzaveta Umarova (Lisa)

Hi! My name is Lisa. I am from Ukraine. Wales was my first destination in the UK, and it became my second home. This monologue helped me to describe my feelings about Wales in detail. I am very grateful for my time here and will always look back to my time in Wales with the smile on my face, and will always be thankful for the opportunity to learn about such a beautiful culture with kindhearted people.